Whisper...
Faith, Love, Self-Care and Healing

Dr Jules

Whisper...
Faith, Love, Self-Care and Healing

©2022 DrJules Brice

ISBN: 978-1-66786-505-8

Editor: Barbara Fant
Cover Design and Layout: Cityboy Studios
Photo Credit: Quianna and Kendall Simpson

Dedication

For my heavenly angels Mom and Tatum

Forward

"Wisdom calls out in the street; she raises her voice in the public squares. She cries out above the commotion; she speaks at the entrance of the city gates," says Proverbs 2:20. In this collection of writings Dr Jules takes us through her process of wisdom. She lifts the veil on her innermost thoughts and offers them to her readers through what feels like her prayers, psalms, and poems.

I had the incredible opportunity of witnessing this collection of writings in its first stages and was blessed enough to experience it become what it is today. Although Dr Jules and I had known each other through mutual friends in the community, my first real conversation with her was when I was in town and was invited to come to her home to meet my mentor, who happened to be dining at her house that evening. She welcomed me in, offered me footies, so that I would be comfortable when I took off my shoes, and she offered me a meal. It was a warm and thoughtful embrace, a loving hug extended to someone she did not quite know. When I open the pages of her collection, I feel that same exact warmth and love that she extended to me on that evening. It is this same love and warmth that she exudes and extends to her readers.

This collection feels like a "welcome home," a home-cooked meal, advice from your mother and auntie, and a mirror showing you your reflection, all in the same breath. What I love most about this collection of writings is that you get to go on a journey with DrJules, learning her thought process, trials, triumphs, moments of falling in love, moments of heartache, the celebration of life, and the processing of life lost, fears and frustration, and the fire-filled faith that guides her life. In experiencing her thought process along her journey, we as readers are offered an opportunity to process through our own emotions in a refreshed way. Through her collection, she offers us a new way; a new way of seeing the world, a new way of experiencing life, and a new way of walking out the journey, and all the wisdom you collect along the way.

In Chapter 3 of Proverbs, the author goes on to say, "Happy is a man who finds wisdom and who acquires understanding.... She is a tree of life to those who embrace her, and those who hold on to her are happy." In this collection of writings, DrJules offers us a tree of life. All we need to do is embrace the love, authenticity, and healing, that she has poured out onto these pages. Our peace, our joy, our happiness is there; all we need to do is receive.

Barbara Fant, MFA, MTS
Author of Mouths of Garden

Acknowledgement

Through the years, I have always had a thought or word of inspiration to share however I found it most comfortable to put pen to paper than saying it aloud. Some 20 years ago, my beautiful mother, Annie L. Brice encouraged me to share my writings with the world. What she saw in me was not more than just her daughter but a writer with words that could impact someone's mind, body, and soul with inspiration. She saw in my what I had not yet realized and even know stand in disbelief that this book is happening.

Mom it is because of your belief and encouragement that I open myself to the world with the first of many writings. I pray for continued strength and encouragement from above and God's unmeasurable blessings.

WHISPER...

Whisper...

Just as loud noise can make your blood run cold and stop you in your tracks instantly, a whisper has the same power but oftentimes just not instantly. A whisper penetrates your soul and is nurtured by life until one day the whisper grows into the knowledge and wisdom that manifest a change in your perspective about past, current, and future experiences. Never underestimate the power and importance of the noise that comes as a whisper.

Whisper...

HEALING

SELF-CARE

LOVE

FAITH

FAITH

Every idea can be good. There just needs to be good planning and thoughtful execution.

Like Joshua and the wall of Jericho, three things happen when you circle an issue:

1. Fear and Doubt decrease
2. Faith and Hope increase
3. Expectation grows

Walk around the issue a few times to expose the weakness, enhance your knowledge, and ensure victory.

Smiling when you're happy makes your face hurt.

Smiling when you're sad makes your soul feel better.

But praising and laughing while crying, now that will get you through.

The hardest things for us to do are to:

Trust God at His work;
Believe that He will make a way;
Wait on His promise; and
Be still until He completes the process

Maybe God wants me to meet a few wrong people before I meet the right one. That way, when I finally meet the right person, I will be grateful for the gift that they are.

There will be times in life when the only encouragement is an act of silence. Silence is a way to hear clearly from God so that you can make a sound decision. Today, I will be silent, so I can hear.

It is not your past, but your press toward wholeness that matters in life.

Have the kind of faith that will allow you to trust God with all your might. Have the kind of faith that will allow you to leap into the fire when you are close, knowing that you will not be consumed.

Our ability to understand God's perspective is complex because our thoughts are minuscule to the mind of God.

God gives us a heart to be comforted, a spirit to be calmed, and faith to be tested.

Not everyone gets burned.
Leap into the fire.

$$\overline{LOVE}$$

It hurts to love someone and to not be loved in return. But what is more painful is to love someone and never find the courage to let them know how you really feel.

If I could make someone smile, who would it be?

If I could make someone happy, who should it be?

If I could help someone replace pain with a love so true,

I think the only one worthy is you.

Before emotion gets involved, resolve the matter.

For love, sometimes you must allow the fire to burn itself out; whatever is found in the aftermath is worth keeping.

Black, Smoove, tender, kind, gentle, warm, strong, adventurous, intelligent, brave, sexy, fun...the makings of you.

Sometimes it's hard to recognize a good thing until you have lost it. It's also hard to recognize a good thing when it arrives.

The happiest people don't necessarily have the best things, unapologetically they make the most of what they do have,

I think of you and wonder, do you ever think of me?

I think of you and wonder when you look at me, what is it you see?

I think of you and wonder, will we ever share the same dream?

I think of you and know it would take forever to redeem all the time I've spent wondering, do you ever think of me?

Loving someone is allowing them to be themselves and not twisting them into the image you want them to be.

Life begins with a smile, grows with a kiss, and ends with a tear.

Enjoy the married life; it's a free ticket to the amusement park.

But you should only ride the rides you both enjoy the most.

Don't try the bungee jump, it's too risky.

The water rides are okay and great if you need to hide tears.

The scream machine is necessary, especially during difficult moments.

The demon drop is a setup. Stay away from it. Once you start falling, it takes twice the effort to get back up.

Now the merry-go-round is perfect; you just keep going around and around, and each time you notice something different — refresh and renew your relationship every day.

If you're wondering what to do with your spare time, invest it in your children. They are a true reflection of how you invest your time.

Love is when you take away the feelings, the passion, and the romance in a relationship and you realize that you still have a benevolent concern for that person.

The essence of you is printed indelibly in my heart.

The feel of your skin indelibly on my fingertips.

The softness of your kisses indelibly on my lips.

The pleasant smell of your scent indelibly in my nose.

The firmness of your arms indelibly around my waist.

The beauty of your face indelibly in my mind.

The sound of your words and laugh indelibly in my ears.

The warmth of your touch indelibly on my face.

You have been indelibly printed in my life.

The wrong we do to one another is not easily forgotten,
but God is able to forgive us in the blink of an eye.

Appreciate the importance of people who have touched your life

Unless you have an added advantage stored in your future, you should begin training your children on the value of the dollar while they are young.

Essential to sisterhood is communication, forgiveness, respect, self-love, trust and accepting who we are together as one.

SELF-CARE

Everyone should experience love, peace, and joy and be active in every aspect of their lives. For to know and not do is the act of murder on future possibilities. You can't kill the dream and not kill the dreamer for they are synonymous.

When you leave a bad situation, go far enough away that the thought of turning around makes no sense at all.

Don't let anyone cover up your light. Let the world will see it radiates from you.

When inheriting someone's crazy, without proper understanding, their crazy might just drive you crazy.

You can't go into someone's kitchen and move the salt and pepper to another cabinet any more than you can change the direction of their toilet paper from under to over. It was their decision to make.

Make sure that the moments you lose are the moments you choose.

Leaving has never been hard. It's what we try to carry with us that is too heavy, keeping us from making it very far.

Building your success on the shoulders of those you consider to be less than you, may not leave you still standing in the end.

If you choose to wear many hats, you may be choosing to take lots of medicine.

Specify.
Clarify.
Define.

We lose ourselves to darkness when we deny
ourselves joy.

What would I say to myself if I never fought on my own behalf?

What would I say to myself if I had given up on possibilities?

What would I say to myself if my heart no longer sung of joy?

What would I say to myself if I could no longer dream?

What would I say to myself if I allowed hurt to continue to direct my path?

I would say:

Fight for what you want.

Accept only what you deserve.

Don't quit.

Keep singing (even a sad song has purpose).

Dreams really do come true.

I forgive and love myself.

The best word for maintaining self-care
is to simply say, No.

Filling your plate with everyone else's thoughts and opinions will still leave you empty. Don't consume the crap that everyone else puts on your plate.

Strength is not allowing your decisions to be weakened by the negativity surrounding the circumstances.

Listening is the key to productivity. Listening is the greatest part of learning. Listening is the path to understanding.

HEALING

Be a part of finding your own solution.

What you are doing right now will determine your position in your next great moment.

Never say never because you might still have some "try" left in you to fight.

If you focus so much on your failures, how can you focus on building your bright future?

After the hurting, crying, and searching has ended, there is true happiness and the chance to try again.

The Whole Story

In the beginning...

...and then there was peace.

The End

Your afflictions may affect your attitude, but they do not excuse your attitude.

Holding on to failure slows down recovery. Healing can't start until you let go of the pain, hold on to hope, and stand firm stand in trust.

There is a reason you have two trash bins: one for garbage and one for recycling. Be careful to sort the trash in your life properly.

Sometimes you need to hear the silence before you can get the message.

Being totally self-centered will separate you from those who care about you and leave you at the mercy of God.

Trust yourself again, but this time, use the knowledge that you have gained to help you not repeat your past.

Broken pieces can be put back together.
Shattered pieces cannot be restored.
Knowing the difference will bring peace.

If you can go back, you have not gone far enough.

Thank You

I would also like to thank my children for their support and for trusting me to be their mom. I'm blessed that not only do you love me but that you are in love with me. Trust me there is a difference.

I'd like to thank my siblings, family, friends, and SisterGirls, LTD. To my sister-friend Suzan C. Bradford your love and support for more than 40 years will never be forgotten and will always in all-way be a guiding light. Special thanks to "the poet" Barbara Fant for your time, patience, and insight that has turned these words into a book of inspiration for some, if not many. Most important thanks to God for placing such wonderful people in my life to assist me with reaching the pivotal moment in my life.

To God be the glory!

About the Author

DrJules is a writer of poems, cards, inspirational messages, and children's stories. DrJules' desire to start writing began long before, marriage, children, education, and career took shape. When her relationship began crumbling, the loss of her mother, health issue, and the sudden death of her son, the broken pieces of her life began to reshape, she began to reimagine her thoughts and dreams of becoming a published writer.

She is an illuminating example of courage through faith and believes that challenges are necessary to develop a stronger inter-self – but one must be willing to - learn from past experiences, make intentional changes, leave negative spaces, take the limits off possibilities and do it all unapologetically.

She has received numerous educational degrees, certifications, and accolades from higher learning institutions, community colleges, and community outreach programs and holds certifications in church ministry and grief counseling. Her experiences have afforded her learning opportunities that impact her inspirational messages whenever she engages with her audience. She is a woman of spiritual belief, passion, vision, and purpose and uses her writing to share her talents with others.

Dr Jules is a transplant from the state of Alabama. Her goal is to use her platform to facilitate healing, growth, and spiritual development using the art of writing books, cards, and poems, making appearances, and gaining a social media platform.